WORLD ALMANAC® LIBRARY
OF THE
AMERICAN REVOLUTION

Daily Life
During the American Revolution

Dale Anderson

WORLD ALMANAC® LIBRARY

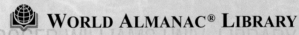

{handwritten: ## 65043168}   {handwritten: 1/07}

Please visit our web site at: www.worldalmanaclibrary.com
For a free color catalog describing World Almanac® Library's list of high-quality books
and multimedia programs, call 1-800-848-2928 (USA) or 1-800-387-3178 (Canada).
World Almanac® Library's fax: (414) 332-3567.

Library of Congress Cataloging-in-Publication Data

Anderson, Dale, 1953-
     Daily life during the American Revolution / by Dale Anderson.
        p. cm. — (World Almanac Library of the American Revolution)
     Includes bibliographical references and index.
     ISBN 0-8368-5930-8 (lib. bdg.)
     ISBN 0-8368-5939-1 (softcover)
     1. United States—History—Revolution, 1775-1783—Social aspects—Juvenile literature.
2. United States—Social conditions—To 1865—Juvenile literature. 3. United States—Social life
and customs—1775-1783—Juvenile literature. I. Title. II. Series.
     E209.A525   2005
     973.3—dc22   2005043585

First published in 2006 by
World Almanac® Library
A Member of the WRC Media Family of Companies
330 West Olive Street, Suite 100
Milwaukee, WI 53212 USA

Produced by Discovery Books
Editor: Sabrina Crewe
Designer and page production: Sabine Beaupré
Photo researcher: Sabrina Crewe
Maps and diagrams: Stefan Chabluk
Consultant: Andrew Frank, Assistant Professor of History, Florida Atlantic University
World Almanac® Library editorial direction: Mark J. Sachner
World Almanac® Library editor: Alan Wachtel
World Almanac® Library art direction: Tammy West
World Almanac® Library production: Jessica Morris

Photo credits: CORBIS: p. 14; The Granger Collection: cover, pp. 17, 19, 20, 24, 27, 28, 29, 31, 37, 39, 43;
Independence National Historical Park: title page; Library of Congress: pp. 7, 11, 22, 35; National Park Service:
p. 25; North Wind Picture Archives: pp. 5, 8, 9, 12, 15, 23, 33, 38, 41.

Printed in Canada

1 2 3 4 5 6 7 8 9 09 08 07 06 05

*Front cover: In 1777, Catherine Schuyler, wife of an American general, set fire to her family's cornfields near Saratoga,
New York, as the British army approached. She took this action to prevent the British soldiers from using the corn.*

*Title page: James Peale painted this portrait of George Washington on horseback in about 1790. He based the
portrait on a work by his brother, Charles Willson Peale—the faces of both the brothers can be seen on the left,
behind Washington. In the background on the right are Revolutionary soldiers, one carrying a French flag.*

Contents

I n 1776, the thirteen British **colonies** along the eastern coast of North America declared themselves independent of Britain. The colonists were already fighting British soldiers in protest at British policies. In 1781, the British surrendered to American forces, and, in 1783, they formally recognized the colonies' independence.

A New Nation

The movement from colonies to independence, known as the American Revolution, gave birth to a new nation—the United States of America. Eventually, the nation stretched to the Pacific Ocean and grew to comprise fifty states. Over time, it was transformed from a nation of farmers into an industrial and technological giant, the world's richest and most powerful country.

An Inspiration to Others

The American Revolution was based on a revolution of ideas. The people who led the American Revolution believed that the purpose of government was to serve the people, not the reverse. They rejected rule by monarchs and created in its place a republic. The founders of the republic later wrote a **constitution** that set up this form of government and guaranteed people's basic rights, including the right to speak their minds and the freedom to worship as they wished.

The ideals on which the United States of America was founded have inspired people all around the world ever since. Within a few years of the American Revolution, the people of France had risen up against their monarchy. Over time, the people of colonies in Central

During the American Revolution, women sometimes had to defend their homes against attack. This print shows a woman armed in preparation for protecting her home and family.

and South America, in Asia, and in Africa followed the U.S. example and rebelled against their position as colonists. Many former colonies have become independent nations.

Life Goes On

While the American Revolution raged, daily life and work had to continue. Major campaigns by large armies generally took place in just one or two places at a time. Eventually, however, the years of war did scar many regions. Large armies and small raiding parties left farms ravaged and cities damaged.

The Revolution also disrupted the **economy**. The British navy **blockaded** the Atlantic coast to prevent the rebellious Americans from selling their goods overseas and receiving supplies from abroad. Daily life continued, however, partly because women took on more economic responsibility. While husbands and fathers were away fighting, women ran the country's farms and businesses. Some drew on that experience—and on the Revolution's ideals of equality and natural rights—to call for more equality between men and women.

Trouble and Disappointments

"I look for you almost every day but I don't allow myself to depend on any thing for I find there is nothing to be depended on but trouble and disappointments."

Letter from Sarah Hodgkins of Massachusetts to her soldier husband during the American Revolution

CHAPTER ONE

The Impact of War on Society

While armies struggled in the field, farmers planted and harvested crops and milked their cows. Craftspeople made barrels, pots and pans, and shoes; storekeepers sold goods; and innkeepers fed and housed travelers. The war, however, had an impact on daily life and brought economic problems that touched all Americans.

Inflation

The American colonies had prospered before the war, but the Revolution jolted their economy. The most serious economic problem was **inflation**, which caused a steep rise in prices.

The Continental **Congress** was the acting government of the new nation during the Revolution. It was made up of representatives from each colony who met to make decisions about how to run the war and to plan for the future. To raise money to pay for the war, the Congress printed paper money. Paper money, in theory, had value because it was backed by government assets, such as gold or silver. This backing meant people who used paper money for exchange of goods could trust it. The Continental dollar, however, was not backed by any such assets, and the value of the money dropped. In 1777, it took $3 in Continentals to buy what $1 of gold or silver would. By 1780, $100 in Continentals was needed to buy goods worth $1. The following year, after the value of the Continental bills had fallen even further, people stopped accepting them.

Shortages

Another factor contributed to inflation—shortages of many everyday items. Fighting disrupted the production of grain for bread and of leather for shoes. The British naval blockade slowed the **importation** of tea, sugar, and other goods. Scarcity, coupled with inflation, drove up prices. A bag of salt costing $1 in 1777 cost $3,900 in 1780. Some states tried to set the prices of basic goods, but merchants, farmers, and craftspeople refused to cooperate. They held onto their goods until they found someone willing to pay higher prices.

Decline in Trade and Production

War also led to recession, or a decline in production of goods. In addition, the British blockade prevented American raw materials from being **exported** to Europe. Industries badly affected included fishing, tobacco, and indigo (a blue dye). All three had been part of a flourishing export trade before the war. Shipping and related industries were also affected. The decline in trade cost many people their jobs.

Eighteen Pence. To counterfeit is *Death.*

Burlington in NEW-JERSEY, Printed by Isaac Collins, 1776.

Farmers generally fared better than other people because the demand for food continued to be high. Some merchants managed to break through the blockade and ship food overseas to markets in southern Europe and the West Indies, but this was a risky practice for merchants and shippers.

7

Political Changes

As the American Revolution progressed, it changed the balance of political power in America. The colonial **legislatures** always had been dominated by men who lived in the largest cities and long-established settlements along the coast. Many of these Easterners, however, were **Loyalists** who supported British rule. So the **Patriots**, hoping to outvote the Loyalists, sought the support of the more independently minded farmers on the western **frontiers**.

Religious Changes

The Revolution brought about changes in American religious life. Before the war, most colonies had an official church, and all citizens paid taxes to support the church even if they did not attend services. In Virginia, the Church of England was the official church. After independence was declared, Virginia's Anglicans (members of the Church of England) formed a new church—the Protestant Episcopal Church of America.

Episcopalians then banded together with Baptists and Presbyterians in Virginia to fight for independence. This common cause made it illogical for the government to support only one church. In 1776, when Patriots in Virginia issued a Declaration of Rights, they took a step toward separation of church and state.

In New Hampshire, Massachusetts, and Connecticut, the Congregationalist Church continued to be supported by taxes until the 1830s. Still, the governments of those states did pass new laws that allowed for government support for Baptist and Methodist churches as well, taking a step away from state approval of only one church. Other states, including Rhode Island, New York, New Jersey, and Pennsylvania, had no official church anyway.

Virginians gather outside Christ Church in Alexandria.

During the Revolution, people from these backcountry areas began to send representatives to the conventions formed to declare independence and create new state governments. People from frontier regions had gained a voice in government for the first time. They were generally people with less wealth and property than those who had served before. They were therefore more likely to support laws benefiting common people.

Oppose Oppression

"Oppose everything that leans to aristocracy or power in the hands of the rich and chief men exercised to the oppression of the poor."

People of Mecklenburg County, North Carolina, instructions to delegates to the Continental Congress

Craft Associations

Among the strongest promoters of rights for common people were craft associations. Craftsmen had had associations for decades, but in the 1770s these groups began to work for the economic and political interests of their members. Associations, or guilds, set standards and prices for their industries. Some, such as the Carpenters' Company of Philadelphia, followed the British tradition of helping those in need and providing education or training.

Groups of carpenters, shoemakers, and blacksmiths also took part in the fight for independence by joining the Patriots. And after independence, many more craft associations appeared.

The Carpenters' Company, founded in 1724, built Carpenters' Hall in Philadelphia in the early 1770s. As well as being the home of the association, the hall (above) was used for the First Continental Congress in 1775.

9

CHAPTER TWO

Life in Town and Country

Wherever armies lived, traveled through, and fought, they brought damage and destruction with them. Battles scarred the land, and hungry troops took crops and livestock to feed themselves. Cities, towns, frontier settlements, and Native American villages were all targets for attacks. The attacks led to widespread destruction, leaving many people without homes.

Fire and Destruction

Several cities were devastated by the war. British **shelling** produced fires that almost completely burned Charlestown, Massachusetts, during the Battle of Bunker Hill in June 1775. Charleston, South Carolina, was badly battered by British forces before the Patriot **garrison** there surrendered in 1780.

Sometimes, destruction was not the result of a direct attack. On September 21, 1776, just after the British army **occupied** New York City, a number of fires broke out in the city. Hundreds of houses and other buildings burned down. There was evidence that the fires had been set deliberately, and the British were convinced that Patriots had set the fires. The occupying British soldiers killed many suspects.

A second fire in 1778 destroyed more property, and, for the rest of the war, living conditions in New York City were poor for British troops and for the thousands of Loyalists who flocked to the city seeking protection. Many families created shelters by stretching sail canvas as a roof over the ruins of buildings where partial walls and chimneys still stood.

On September 19, 1776, fire devastated New York City. This print from the 1770s shows the British soldiers who occupied the city beating citizens as flames raged through buildings.

Under Siege

Cities that were occupied or under **siege** by an army suffered badly. Overcrowding—combined with lack of food, clean water, and sanitation—created a breeding ground for disease. Patriots held British troops under siege in Boston for nearly a year until the British left the city in March 1776. Unhealthy conditions led to **epidemics** of dysentery and smallpox that ravaged the city and spread through New England. Philadelphia, also occupied by the British, had a smallpox outbreak in 1777.

The overall population of America's city and towns declined during the war. This was partly due to the decline in trade and production, which forced thousands to leave cities to look for work on farms and in small villages. Thousands of men left to join the armies, too. The threat of war also reduced city populations—many people fled when an army was approaching. Women with children and elderly people left to stay with family or friends in the country.

Taking Over Property

Some people, of course, remained in their homes to defend their property or because they had nowhere to go. They lived in fear of being caught in

Even before the first battles of the American Revolution had been fought, British soldiers arrived in Boston in large numbers because of unrest in the city. Troops were sent to live in people's houses against the homeowners' wishes.

the fighting or of having their property destroyed.

When the British army occupied a city, it took over houses and public buildings for its own use. Officers installed themselves in the houses of the wealthy; soldiers lived in the homes of ordinary people. Soldiers seized clothing, food, animal feed, and personal possessions. They often destroyed what they could not use.

When they occupied Boston, the British used many churches for military purposes. One was turned into a riding school, and several others served as barns. Some were converted into **barracks**. Houses, churches, and fences were torn down and used for firewood. After the army **evacuated**, returning residents whose homes still stood found their property dirty, damaged, and full of garbage and waste.

License to Plunder

"[British troops] think they have a license to plunder every one's house and store who leaves the town."

Merchant John Andrews, describing life in Boston during the British occupation, 1775

Moving In

Some houses occupied by soldiers were being lived in, generally by women and children whose men were away fighting. Soldiers moved in with families, taking over living areas and main bedrooms and forcing the families to live in just a fraction of their own homes. The British often treated the families abusively. Many women afterward complained of the soldiers' wild parties, drinking, and unruliness. They worried about how this behavior might affect their young children.

Women also worried about the threat of rape. A few soldiers took advantage of the fact that the men were away fighting, leaving women relatively defenseless. It was not only the British who raped women, however. Patriot soldiers sometimes attacked Loyalist women, too.

Poverty and Wealth

The poor suffered more than others in the cities. Although they had fewer possessions to lose, they found it harder to pay the inflated prices charged for food and other necessities during the war. Many poor people lost their jobs or businesses as a result of the Revolution.

At the other end of the scale, British officers and wealthy Loyalists maintained an active social life in occupied cities. During the British occupation of Philadelphia, there were weekly balls and frequent concerts, dinners, parties, and plays. Similar activities took place in New York City, where officers performed in theatrical events. In areas held by the Continental army—the army formed by the Congress—wealthy Patriots socialized with Continental officers. During the winter months, when

The *Mischianza*

Late in the winter of 1777–1778, the British accepted General William Howe's request to resign from overall command of the British forces in America. In the spring of 1778, before he left Philadelphia for Britain, the general's staff gave him a farewell party. They called it the *Mischianza*, or "Medley." More than seven hundred guests were invited to this extravagant affair. British officers and Loyalists enjoyed not only dinner and dancing, but fabulous entertainment. Gun salutes were fired from barges on the river, and a medieval tournament was fought between two groups of officers pretending to be knights.

In 1776, the British army, along with a large number of Loyalists, left Boston. The city was left damaged and disrupted by the occupation.

Under Our Roofs

"[W]e have trying and grievous scenes to go through; fighting, brawls, drumming and **fifing**, and dancing the night long; card and dice playing, and every abomination going on under our very roofs."

Lydia Mintern Post, civilian
whose house was taken over by British soldiers,
Long Island, New York

little fighting took place, they held dances, card parties, and concerts.

The War in Different Regions

At the start of the war, people in New England saw many hardships. After British troops evacuated Boston in 1776, however, conditions in that area improved. Most New Englanders lived out the rest of the war in relative peace, although coastal areas remained open to raids. The British raided parts of Connecticut in 1777, 1779, and 1781. The towns of Danbury, Fairfield,

Norwalk, and New London were largely burned down in these strikes.

The South had its worst period after 1778, when major fighting began there. In general, however, **civilians** in New York, Pennsylvania, and New Jersey suffered the most. As both armies moved around the country between 1776 and 1783, disorderly troops spread havoc.

Abigail Adams (1744–1818)

Witty, well read, and respected by those who met her, Abigail Smith Adams was the wife of the second U.S. president, John Adams, and mother of the sixth, John Quincy Adams. She was born in Massachusetts, daughter of a Congregational minister, and married John Adams in 1764.

During the British occupation of Boston in 1775 and 1776, Adams gave food and shelter to people fleeing the city and to passing Patriot soldiers. Despite fear that fighting might reach her door, she decided to stay in her home. Adams managed the family farm and business affairs and raised her children throughout the war while her husband served in the Continental Congress. An early and staunch supporter of independence, Abigail Adams believed slavery was against the principles Americans were fighting for. She also supported the rights of women, particularly the right to an education. Adams urged her husband to convince the Congress to recognize the rights of women when making laws for the new country.

In 1784, Adams left to join her husband in France, where he was negotiating peace with the British. The couple then moved to London, where John Adams became the U.S. ambassador. The Adamses returned to Massachusetts in 1788, but not for long—John Adams became U.S. vice president in 1789 and then president in 1797. The couple retired to Massachusetts in 1801.

Philadelphia and New York

Philadelphia fared better under occupation than Boston. Bands of Patriots or Continental army patrols sometimes stopped farmers from taking produce into the city, but most people inside did not lack food or firewood. City dwellers could even find some luxuries. One Philadelphia businessman had enough wealthy customers to be able to sell silk knee garters and satin cloth.

New York City was the headquarters of the British army from September of 1776 until November 1783. With thousands of Loyalists, thousands more soldiers, and ships frequently arriving from Britain, the city was bustling. Farms in the surrounding area supplied the city with food, fuel, and animal feed, but not enough for its large population. The extremely cold and snowy winters of the period sometimes made it difficult to bring in supplies.

Looting the Countryside

In the countryside, armies on both sides **looted** and destroyed property and—occasionally—killed civilians. Soldiers stole sometimes out of necessity and at other times just for sport. After battles, they often entered empty houses to loot what they could find.

Commanders of both armies objected to the looting and mistreatment of civilians and took steps to stop it. Patriot commander George Washington and British generals William Howe and Henry Clinton had officers search their men after battles. Soldiers who murdered civilians were hanged by both armies, and thieves were forced to return stolen property. Most were not caught, however, and the abuses continued throughout the war.

Brigands

Sometimes these crimes were committed not by soldiers, but by bands of thieves, or **brigands**, who moved to an area after an army left. They stole everything—furniture, clothes, food, and the carts and horses to carry them off. Brigands were particularly common in the South. The troops hated being blamed for the brigands' crimes. In South Carolina, Patriot **militia** leader Francis Marion gave his men

Havoc

"[The] havoc is not to be described. Great numbers of women and children have been left without a second shift of clothes. The furniture which [the looters] could not carry off they wantonly broke, burnt, and destroyed."

Patriot Oliver Hart, letter describing looting in the South, 1779

permission to shoot brigands without waiting for a trial.

Indian Raids

Frontier areas in the North and the South saw frequent raids, which often involved Native Americans. In western New York, Loyalists and their Iroquois allies attacked Patriot settlements throughout the war. In 1779, General John Sullivan led a Patriot force that took revenge on Native American attackers. His soldiers destroyed forty Iroquois towns along with the Indians' crops and orchards. Similar strikes and counterstrikes took place in other areas, leaving the people in frontier regions always uneasy.

On July 3, 1778, communities in Wyoming Valley, Pennsylvania, were attacked by Loyalist and Native American troops. Many men, women, and children were brutally killed.

CHAPTER THREE

Women in the War

A handful of women saw the war firsthand when they disguised themselves as men and joined the army to fight. Many more were camp followers, meaning they marched and camped along with their soldier husbands. Other women were spies. The vast majority of women, however, spent the war at home, where they shouldered many new burdens. They met these demands while worrying about their husbands in the army and fearing what might happen to them and their children if war came to their doors.

The Colonial Household

Among American colonists, fathers and husbands had all the authority in the home. The man led the household and had the right to make all major decisions affecting family members. Marriage was the natural goal for a woman. Once daughters married, they shifted their obedience from their fathers to their husbands. Women who remained unmarried had little social status.

Dutiful Wife and Daughter

"You have been a dutiful child to your parents. Your natural disposition will in like manner incline you to be dutiful and affectionate to your husband and his parents. . . . Let your dress, your conversation, and the whole business of your life be to please your husband and to make him happy and you need not fail of being so yourself."

Cadwallader Colden, botanist, doctor, and New York politician, letter to his daughter, 1737

A household scene at the time of the Revolution shows women cooking, churning butter, and spinning.

Most white colonial women married in their early twenties, and they usually gave birth to six or seven children. Child rearing took up a great deal of time, and there was much other work as well. Women cooked and cleaned, of course, but they also produced many of the items needed in the home—clothing, candles, and soap; butter, cheese, and cider; preserved meats, fruits, and vegetables. Women in the South who lived on plantations also supervised the feeding, clothing, and housing of slaves.

Rights and Responsibilities

Although they had many responsibilities, white colonial women had few rights. Husbands controlled the property of wives. That included land and goods that the woman's family gave her when she married. It also included any income she earned by working. Women could not sign contracts on their own, nor were they allowed to bring a lawsuit against another person. Divorce was extremely rare.

The war placed new demands on women. One South Carolina woman

Women, particularly those in isolated areas, had to shoulder many responsibilities during the Revolution. People on remote farms, such as the one above, had no resources except a small area of land and their own hard work.

Cares of Many Kinds

"I have to think and provide every thing for my family, at a time when it is so difficult to provide anything, at almost any price, and cares of many kinds . . . engage my attention."

Pennsylvania Quaker Sally Fisher, diary entry, 1775

wrote, "A soldier made is a farmer lost." But someone had to do the work of that lost farmer, and so the work fell on women who remained at home. They had to do more than just plow, plant, weed, and harvest. Women also had to make business decisions about what to plant, when to harvest, and what to sell the crop for.

Some women felt overwhelmed by their new responsibilities. Mary Foster of Massachusetts wrote her husband:

20

"Every trouble however trifling I feel with double weight in your absence." Others adopted their new roles gladly, or at least with grim determination.

Taking Charge

At first, women often relied on the advice of older men who had not left for the army. As the war continued, however, these women became more experienced in handling affairs. Their husbands often accepted that they should exercise their own judgment in making key decisions. "I can't give any other directions about home," one soldier husband wrote, "but must leave all to your good management." Indeed, many women proved themselves skilled at managing the family economy.

Women's active roles made them feel more a part of the family business than they had before. In her first letters to her husband, Mary Bartlett wrote of "your farming business." Two years later, she called it "our farming business." In some families, wives continued to play a more active role in family business after the war. Once they had demonstrated to themselves—and their husbands—that they were capable of handling such matters, many women were unwilling to give complete control of business affairs to their husbands. Some men were able to adapt. Timothy Pickering of Pennsylvania

Sarah Hodgkins's Letters

The letters written by Sarah Hodgkins to her soldier husband Joseph reflect the feelings of many wives. Joseph served in the Massachusetts militia starting in April 1775, when their youngest child was but a month old. Late that year, Sarah lamented that she had "a sweet babe almost six months old but have got no father for it." In another letter, she told Joseph that her heart "ached" for him, and she wrote, "I want to see you" countless times. In 1776, Joseph reenlisted for three more years over his wife's protests. Sarah worried about his safety but in the end showed resignation: "All I can do for you," she wrote, "is to commit you to God."

wrote his wife approvingly of the change: "This war which has so often and long separated us has taught me how to value you."

Trembling with Terror

"I trembled so with terror, that I could not support myself. . . . We could neither eat, drink, nor sleep in peace; for as we lay in our clothes every night, we could not enjoy the little sleep we got. . . . Our nights were wearisome and painful; our days spent in anxiety and melancholy."

Eliza Wilkinson of South Carolina, describing how she felt after British troops robbed the family home, 1782

Loneliness and Fear

Living apart from soldier husbands, of course, was a strain for many women. Many eased that strain by maintaining close friendships with other women, sharing their worries and fears.

Life was even more challenging and lonely for Loyalist women than for Patriots. They had to suffer not only separation

Children of working families did not always attend school on a regular basis, but many learned to read and write at home. This 1779 primer belonged to a young Connecticut girl.

from their husbands, but also—if they lived in Patriot communities—being shunned by their neighbors and former friends. (These difficulties were sometimes shared by Patriot women living in Loyalist communities.) Some Loyalist women moved to Britain or to other British colonies during the war for safety. There, they were cut off from their own people and the country they had grown up in. One Loyalist woman living in Scotland wrote painfully that she felt herself a "stranger" with no hope of earning money, as she knew no one.

Along with the loneliness, many women—both Patriot and Loyalist—faced anxiety. They were afraid of attacks on themselves, their children, and their homes by enemy troops or brigands. And they deeply feared what might happen to their husbands, fathers, or sons off at war.

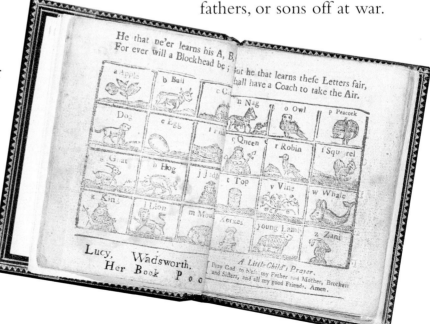

Children and the War

Young children were another responsibility for those mothers who had to tend to household chores and a farm or business. On the other hand, mothers developed close relationships with their children in wartime.

Boys and girls helped with household and farm or business chores from a young age. In this respect, children's lives during the war did not differ much from their experience before the war. Girls could help with cooking and cleaning and, on farms, perform such tasks as milking cows, collecting eggs, and feeding chickens. Even before the war, farm boys worked in the fields.

One change brought on by the war was in the source of parental authority. In colonial America, fathers had complete control over children. In their absence, mothers took on greater authority.

Children were expected to work in colonial and revolutionary times. This print shows a young girl on a family farm bringing in cows from the pasture.

Helping the Cause

Women had been important contributors to the Patriot cause before the war. In the late 1760s and early 1770s, many colonists had protested British **taxes** on goods imported into the

Spies and Saviors

Besides keeping the economy going by raising food and tending to businesses, women helped the war effort in countless ways. Some acted as spies, either on a regular basis or on a single occasion when they had the opportunity to pass information to the side they favored.

Other women performed acts that saved lives. Harriet Pinckney, in South Carolina, saved the Patriot leader Francis Marion from British troops pursuing him. She showed Marion where he could hide and then delayed the British at her home to allow his escape.

Rebecca Motte, also in South Carolina, sacrificed a

A woman gives information about British troop movements to one of General Washington's officers near Philadelphia in 1777.

family home to the cause. A troop of British soldiers had taken over her house when a Patriot force arrived in the area. The Patriots considered setting the house on fire to drive the British out but feared to deprive Motte, a widow, of her home. She dismissed the concern and told them to go ahead and burn the house.

Knitting Stockings

"The plan laid down for our education was entirely broken in upon by the war. Instead of morning lessons, we were to knit stockings; instead of embroidery to make up homespun garments."

Betsy Ambler Brent, Virginia Patriot,
recalling her childhood during the war

A woman sews a soldier's uniform in a historical reenactment at Fort Stanwix, New York. The fort was the site of conflict during the Revolution.

American colonies. They did this by **boycotting** British goods. Women played active roles in this movement. Indeed, their efforts to replace the goods that used to be imported made it easier for Americans to keep up the boycotts. Women gathered in groups to form "spinning bees," where they spun **flax**, wool, or cotton that could be woven into cloth so that British cloth would no longer be needed. They also dried the leaves of different plants to make teas to replace imported teas.

Similar activities continued during the war. Many women devoted as much time as they could to making clothing for soldiers and did anything else they could to aid the war effort.

A New Interest

The turmoil before and during the war changed the way many women saw their roles. Before the American Revolution, there was a general assumption that women were not capable of understanding politics. The 1770s and 1780s changed that. Women who had never discussed politics now wondered why they should not think about something so important to all Americans. Even some men came to see that women could be interested in politics. This new attitude continued after the war.

CHAPTER FOUR

The Loyalists

Probably no single group suffered more in the war than the Loyalists—the white Americans who remained loyal to the British. (There were many Native Americans and African Americans who took the British side, too, but the term Loyalists is used here to mean British colonists.) Patriot mobs and armies harassed them, and laws passed by Patriot governments took away their rights and their property. Many Loyalists saw friendships and family ties break over the issue of independence.

A Large Minority

Loyalists numbered about one-fifth or so of the whites in the colonies, as many as 500,000 people. At the time, they were called Tories, which was the name of a British political faction that showed strong support for the king. Loyalists —like Patriots—could be found in all regions, although there were relatively few in New England. The middle states of New York, New Jersey, and Pennsylvania, together with South Carolina and Georgia in the South, had the largest numbers of Loyalists.

Harassment by Law

Patriots moved quickly to suppress Loyalists and their views. In 1775 and 1776, as the American Revolution began, Patriots set up new legislatures to govern the states. These legislatures passed laws aimed at identifying and punishing Loyalists. First, the new state governments passed "test laws" that required Americans to swear allegiance to the Patriot cause. Next, they passed laws to hurt those who opposed the Revolution. Pennsylvania passed a law that would punish **treason** with death or confiscation of property. It defined treason in several ways, including joining the British army or giving it information. Another law declared that people who spoke against the Revolution could have half their property seized. There were similar laws in other states.

Loyalists were not allowed to vote in elections or hold office. New regulations denied them the right to bring lawsuits. Indeed, some states prevented Loyalists from practicing law.

Becoming an Outlaw

"Our Assembly have at length in their wisdom, prepared a test act obliging all to vow allegiance to the state and abjure the king; the penalty is, being in effect outlawed."

James Allen, Pennsylvania Loyalist, writing in his diary, 1777

Patriot troops threaten an elderly Loyalist during the Revolution. Laws passed by several legislatures made being a Loyalist a criminal offense.

William Franklin (above left), son of the famous Patriot Benjamin Franklin, was Royal Governor of New Jersey. He remained loyal to the British when the Revolution began and was arrested as a Loyalist in 1776.

Pennsylvania extended these bans to teachers, doctors, and pharmacists.

Laws took away Loyalists' freedom of speech by banning any criticism of the Continental Congress or its worthless paper money. Other laws confined Loyalists to their homes or farms, denying them the right to travel freely. Some laws gave officials the power to exile Loyalists, or force them to leave their homes.

Execution and Punishment

Some Loyalists were simply seized and executed. Pennsylvania charged nearly five hundred people with treason, but only a few were executed. Most fled.

A handful appealed and managed to have their names cleared.

Most executions for treason took place in areas where fighting between Patriots and Loyalists was frequent. Executions of Loyalists were often met with reprisal killings of Patriots.

Shunned

Patriots often refused to do business with Loyalists. One Maryland doctor explained that his practice simply melted away. Some patients abandoned him because they objected to his Loyalist views. Others feared that they themselves would be hurt by Patriots if they sought his treatment.

Losing Property

The Patriots targeted the property of Loyalists that had been wealthy and powerful before the war. Thomas Hutchinson, the royal governor of Massachusetts, was one example. In 1779, the Massachusetts legislature passed a law that labeled Hutchinson and some other Loyalists as "notorious conspirators" and said their property could be taken by the state. The Loyalists' lands and homes would be sold, with one-third going to the men's wives. The rest went to anyone owed money by the Loyalists, and any remainder went to the state treasury.

Joseph Galloway (c. 1731–1803)

Joseph Galloway was born in Maryland. He trained to be a lawyer and started a practice in Philadelphia. Galloway was a close friend of Benjamin Franklin and became active in Pennsylvania politics before the American Revolution.

At the First Continental Congress in 1774, Galloway tried to help settle the growing differences between Americans and the British government. He proposed a plan that would unite the colonies but keep them under the control of the British Parliament. His plan narrowly failed to win approval. As war broke out, Galloway became a Loyalist and refused to serve in the Second Continental Congress, the body that eventually declared independence. The British named him as the civilian administrator of Philadelphia when they occupied the city in 1777. Galloway moved to Britain in 1778. In 1788, the Pennsylvania legislature voted him guilty of treason and ordered that his property be seized. Galloway appealed in the hopes of being able to return to the United States, but his appeal was denied. He died in Britain.

Sometimes, these changes overturned the social order. Loyalist Frederick Philipse held about 50,000 acres (about 20,000 hectares) along the Hudson River north of New York City. Living on Philipse's land were hundreds of tenant farmers who paid him rent to farm the land. When Philipse left America during the war, the New York legislature passed a law giving the tenants the first right to buy part of the land. Nearly three hundred farmers took the opportunity to become landowners.

Peace Negotiations

How to treat the Loyalists was a sticking point in the peace negotiations that took place at the end of the war. The British wanted Loyalists to be allowed to return to the United States and regain their possessions. The U.S. negotiators were unwilling to go that far, thinking that other Americans would not approve. In the end, the negotiators agreed to recommend such measures to the states but not to insist on them. The British gave in. Loyalists, knowing that the state governments would not accept the recommendation, felt betrayed.

The British did, however, set up a commission that aimed to compensate Loyalists for their losses. It received more than four thousand claims and paid out money to compensate people who had lost their homes, their property, and their livelihoods. The British also gave land and supplies to some Loyalist families that resettled in Canada.

After the War

In all, nearly 100,000 Loyalists decided they could not live in an independent United States. Large numbers sailed from New York City in 1782 and 1783 to build new lives elsewhere. Many made this choice unwillingly, fearing they would not be safe if they remained. Some moved to Britain, and some settled in British colonies in the West Indies.

The vast majority of Loyalists moved to Canada, where they had to clear land to build new homes and settlements. Years later, a Loyalist who

Cast Off as Beggars

"My dear sir, Great Britain is ten times more afflicting and cuts deeper to the heart than all the Americans can do to us. We have made them our enemies by adhering to and endeavoring to support the constitution and government of England, for which cause we are slighted and cast off as beggars."

New York Loyalist Beverley Robinson, writing to British general Henry Clinton about the Treaty of Paris, 1783

settled in New Brunswick recalled what he had seen on arriving: "Nothing but wilderness [lay] before our eyes. The women and children did not refrain from tears."

A New Home in Canada

The influx of Loyalists launched a new period in Canadian history. Earlier settlers there had been French and Catholic from the days that the area had been ruled by France. The Loyalists made the colony more British and more Protestant. They labored hard in their new home. Many had been talented leaders

Wishing for America

"I earnestly wish to spend the remainder of my days in America. I love the country, I love the people."

Exiled Loyalist William Pepperell, diary entry, 1778

before the Revolution, and many were driven by the desire to build a society better than the one they had fled. A Canadian historian, writing years later, called the Loyalists "the makers of Canada."

After arriving in Canada, this group of exiled Loyalists from the United States drew lots for parcels of land. The hard work of building farms and settlements lay ahead.

CHAPTER FIVE

African Americans

Patriots proclaimed freedom and equality as their guiding principles, but they denied both to African Americans. Thousands of blacks gained their freedom by escaping their masters and joining the British.

Life During the War

About 500,000 African Americans lived in slavery when the Revolution began. There were some free blacks throughout the colonies as well, but only a small number.

For most slaves, life during the war continued much as before, with many of them working in

Liberty Is a Great Thing

"That liberty is a great thing we know from our own feelings, and we may likewise judge so from the conduct of the white people in the late war. How much money has been spent and how many lives have been lost to defend their liberty! I must say that I have hoped that God would open their eyes, when they were so much engaged for liberty, to think of the state of the poor blacks, and to pity us."

African American Jupiter Hammon, essay on freedom for African Americans, 1787

George Washington, revolutionary leader and first U.S. president, was also a slave owner. This illustration shows him on his Virginia plantation with members of his family and some of his slaves.

the fields of southern landowners. Slaves who worked in homes or businesses also labored as they had before the war. They cooked and cleaned or worked as blacksmiths and carpenters.

Some slaves used what little spare time they had to grow their own food. Most slaves lived in slave quarters, which held several families in poor, sparse conditions. Those who lived on farms had enough food during the war. Those who lived in cities and towns saw smaller rations if their owner's family faced problems due to lack of food or money.

Contradiction

Some people hoped that Patriots would recognize the great contradiction between their ideals of freedom and equality and the status of slaves. Samuel Johnson, a noted British writer, blasted Americans as hypocrites, saying, "How is it that we hear the loudest yelps for liberty among the drivers of negroes?"

Not all Patriots supported slavery. Abigail Adams was, like her husband John Adams, a passionate supporter of independence. She wrote, "I wish most sincerely there was not a slave in the province. It always appeared a most iniquitous scheme to me—[to] fight ourselves for what we are daily robbing and plundering from those who have as good a right to freedom as we have."

Black Patriots

A few African Americans won their freedom by joining Patriot armies, some of them being placed in the army as substitutes for slave owners who did not wish to serve themselves. After the war, Virginia slave owners tried to regain control over their former slaves. Governor Benjamin

Freedom for Loyalty

"There are many negroes who have been very useful. . . . For their loyalty, they have been promised their freedom. . . . [They cannot] in justice be abandoned to the merciless resentment of their former masters."

British general Alexander Leslie, letter to General Guy Carleton, 1782

Harrison got the state legislature to pass a law granting these blacks their freedom, as had been promised.

Fighting for the British

Thousands of blacks gained freedom by running away to the British side. Some of these African Americans fought. Others did various tasks that supported the army—carrying goods, digging, and so on. Blacks often worked as servants or cooks in the army, or they found work in cities occupied by the British army.

Moving On

As the war ended, the British took as many as twenty thousand blacks out of the United States. Some settled in other British colonies in the West Indies. A few African Americans were betrayed when British officers or Loyalists sold them back into slavery and pocketed the proceeds.

Many blacks moved to Florida or Canada and settled there. In Canada, life was not as good as they had hoped. Black settlers found that promised land grants were often delayed or of poor quality. Many had to endure the prejudice of white Loyalists.

About one thousand African Americans agreed in 1791 to move to West Africa, where a British company was starting a new colony for freed slaves. That colony is now the country of Sierra Leone.

Steps to Ban Slavery

In the years after the war, some progress was made in northern states. New Hampshire and Massachusetts banned slavery outright. Connecticut, Pennsylvania, and Rhode Island all passed laws that called for ending slavery gradually, over a period of some years. By 1804, New York and New Jersey had done so as well. But in the South, state governments refused to consider an end to slavery.

Phillis Wheatley (1753–1784)

Born in West Africa, Phillis Wheatley was captured as a child and sent to America to become a slave. She ended up in Boston, where she was purchased as a servant by a family named Wheatley, from whom she got her name. They treated the young girl well and allowed her to learn to read and write. Wheatley even received schooling in Latin and Greek. She began to write poetry, which attracted some attention for its religious and moral messages. In 1773, some of Wheatley's poems were published as *Poems on Various Subjects, Religious and Moral*, the first published volume of poetry by an African American. In 1778, Wheatley was freed from slavery and married John Peters, a free black man in Boston. She worked as a servant until her death at a young age.

This portrait of Phillis Wheatley illustrated her collection of poems.

CHAPTER SIX

Native Americans

T he long-term impact of the Revolution on Native Americans was negative. The winning of American independence launched the westward march of settlement that ultimately resulted in Indians losing their land and self-rule.

Life Away from War

Native Americans—like white Americans—did not spend the entire war fighting. Each region saw peace at different times. In those periods, Native American groups followed their traditional ways of life. Farming peoples of the North and the Southeast grew crops, such as corn, and hunted deer, squirrel, and turkey. Many lived in small villages of a hundred or so people. Iroquois peoples lived in well-built towns with wooden walls surrounding as many as one hundred homes.

The war did slow the trading that linked Native Americans and whites. In the Great Lakes region of the North, Native Americans traded beaver pelts. In the South, they provided deerskins. The British blockade and the general economic slowdown cut whites' demands for these goods.

Choosing Sides

The war affected many Native Americans in other ways. Before the Revolution, the British had tried to limit white settlement west of the Appalachian Mountains. If that policy had continued, Native American life in the West could have gone on as before. Many Native American peoples, therefore, supported the British during the war.

Some tribes, however, resented the British from earlier times. Others concluded that the Americans would win and that it was better to be on friendly terms with the victor. There were groups that agreed to support the Patriots but suffered at their hands. The Delaware and Shawnee peoples of western Pennsylvania were angered when goods promised them were never delivered. Worse, some Patriot troops raided Native American villages in Pennsylvania. In one 1781 attack, the Shawnee town of Coshocton—home to two thousand people—was burned to the ground. The people who lived there fled from the area.

Allied with the British

The Cherokees were active allies of the British. They launched raids against American settlements from North Carolina to Georgia early in

A print of a Mohawk town in about 1780 shows a typical Iroquois community at the time of the Revolution.

The British gave this commemorative medal to their Native allies after the American Revolution. It shows an Indian warrior and British soldier shaking hands under the motto "Happy While United."

Great Discontent

"Brother, listen with great attention. . . . We were greatly alarmed and cast down when we heard the news [of the Treaty of Paris], and it occasions great discontent and surprise with our people. . . . We beg that the King will be put in mind by you and recollect what . . . we have . . . done for him and his subjects."

Joseph Brant, letter to British official Frederick Haldimand, 1783

1776, despite the urgings of the British to avoid a fight. A Patriot counterattack began in August of 1776, destroying several Cherokee villages. Refused help by the British, the Cherokee begged for peace. In treaties signed in May and July of 1777, they gave up all claims to land east of the Appalachians and moved west of the mountains to make new homes.

The Iroquois Confederacy

The Mohawk, Onondaga, Cayuga, Seneca, Oneida, and Tuscarora peoples belonged to an alliance called the Iroquois Confederacy. This union had existed for several hundred years, but the American Revolution nearly destroyed it. The Oneida and Tuscarora sided with the Patriots. The other four allied themselves with the British, and they provided nearly 1,600 fighters to the British war effort. Leading these Loyalist forces in several fights was the Mohawk chief Joseph Brant.

Both the British and Patriots carried out attacks on the Iroquois peoples allied to the other side. In these attacks, Mohawk and Oneida fought each other—the kind of conflict that the confederacy agreement was supposed to prevent.

The six nations remained somewhat divided after the war but once again met in their grand councils. The war broke the power of the Iroquois. The four nations that had

Joseph Brant (1742–1807)

This portrait of Joseph Brant was painted by George Romney in 1776.

Joseph Brant was born in what is now Ohio and attended a white school for Indians in Connecticut. There, he learned English, became a Christian, and began to translate Christian works into the Mohawk language. Throughout his life, Brant remained a Christian missionary. In 1775, Brant became a captain in the British army. When the American Revolution began, he persuaded many of his people to support the British, convinced that they would otherwise lose their lands. Brant took part in several battles in New York. White Americans greatly feared Brant, and the British promoted him to the rank of colonel.

When the war ended, the British handed Native lands west of the United States to the Americans. Brant acquired reservation land in Canada for his people and settled there. He continued his religious translations and his efforts to help Native peoples retain their homelands in the United States.

joined the British moved to new lands in Canada. The Oneida and Tuscarora remained in New York but were forced by Americans to give up their lands in the 1780s. Some settled in Wisconsin, although a fragment of both tribes remained in New York.

Terms of Peace

In the Treaty of Paris of 1783, negotiated at the end of the war, Britain gave the United States all the land east of the Mississippi River except Florida. This was land the British had won from France twenty years earlier, but, for the Native Americans living there, it was their homeland. The huge land grant caused great bitterness among Native people and set the stage for the next few decades of conflict between whites and Native Americans in the United States of America.

CHAPTER SEVEN

The Postwar Years

The war had created an economic decline that continued after the conflict ended. There was political turmoil, too.

Recession

By the end of the Revolution, America's export trade and the businesses that depended on that trade were in ruins. In addition, many American businesses established during the war failed, unable to compete in price with the cheap British goods that were once again being imported. High prices of goods and worthless money caused problems as well. Farmers were hard pressed to make mortgage payments on their land, and, in some areas, banks seized farm property.

These issues helped convince some leaders that it was time to address the country's problems. In 1787, national leaders created a new framework of government, the U.S. Constitution. Time and new government policies helped the economy recover and grow.

Trade and Industry Develops

A couple of economic developments signaled the coming growth. In 1784, a cargo ship carried

Some Crisis

"Our affairs seem to lead to some crisis, some revolution—something I cannot foresee or conjecture. I am uneasy and apprehensive; more so than during the war."

U.S. statesman John Jay, letter to George Washington, 1787

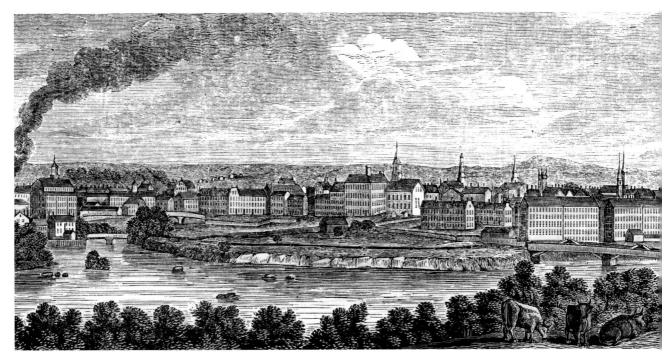

After the Revolution, the cotton industry brought prosperity to growers in the South and textile manufacturers and merchants in the North. Massachusetts became the center of a booming U.S. textile industry. By the early 1800s, textile mills lined the river in Lowell, Massachusetts, shown above.

goods from the United States to China and brought back goods in return. Soon, many ships were sailing the seas to pursue trade with China.

In 1790, Samuel Slater opened the first textile mill in the United States in Pawtucket, Rhode Island, launching the American textile industry. By the mid-1790s, the nation was on the road to growth and prosperity.

Social Changes

Life in the United States was similar in many ways to life in the colonies, but there were differences. People became less willing to accept the distinctions between the wealthy and the poor that had marked colonial society before the war. After all, it was the common people who had helped win independence and ensure that Americans could live free.

As a result, ordinary people pushed for voting rights. At first, only white men who owned property could vote. Gradually, states loosened the property requirement. By the 1820s, most states had extended the right to vote to all white males. Here was a social change indeed, as a much larger percentage of ordinary people came to have a voice in government. The voting rights of women, Native Americans, and African Americans were still ignored.

Women After the War

After the war ended, white women in the United States were seen as having a new responsibility—to raise a generation of virtuous, intelligent children ready to be citizens in a republic. Mothers gained new status as parents. They were allowed to have some influence even on their sons, instead of always deferring to their husbands in child-rearing decisions.

An even more fundamental change in women's thinking took place after the war. By the 1790s, some women were choosing not to marry. Once spinsters (unmarried women) had been scorned, but now many women argued that it was far worse to marry an undesirable man than to be single. The vast majority of women still married, but this change in attitude was a sign of growing independence among women.

Not Worthy of Marrying

"It is much better to remain single than to be badly matched. I know no other reason why so many accomplished girls should be getting old maids except that the young men are not worthy of them."

Nathalie Sumter of South Carolina, writing on marriage after the war

Native Lands

The U.S. victory in the Revolution brought new challenges for Native Americans, as they had feared. After the war, white settlers began pouring into what is now Ohio, an area that offered rich farmland. Native Americans there resisted the new settlers, and fighting broke out in 1791. The combined forces of the Shawnee and Miami defeated U.S. troops led by General Arthur St. Clair in present-day Indiana in November of that year.

General Anthony Wayne was put in charge of a new army. He won several minor battles against Native forces in Ohio in 1793 and a major victory at the Battle of Fallen Timbers in August 1794. In the Treaty of Greenville, signed on August 3, 1795, Native Americans gave up their claim to most of Ohio.

Life in Slavery Goes On

For the vast majority of enslaved African Americans, the Revolution made little difference. Slaves continued to suffer from forced labor and poor living conditions. While northern states decided to ban slavery, the slave population of the South grew. There were about 500,000 slaves in the American colonies when the war broke out. In the first census (or population count) of the United States in 1790, there were nearly 700,000.

Because of the growing cotton industry, slave labor was more important than ever to Southerners. This was an issue that, in the next century, would divide Americans once again and cause an even bloodier war.

Slaves on a southern plantation operate a cotton gin.

The Cotton Gin

A new innovation helped the textile industry grow. In 1793, Eli Whitney introduced the cotton gin, a machine that made it possible for workers to clean seeds out of cotton at a rate far faster than could be done by hand. The invention came at the right time. Southern planters expanded their production of cotton to meet the rising demand of textile mills in Britain and in New England. Cotton production jumped from under 140,000 pounds (63,500 kilograms) in 1792 to 35 million pounds (16 million kg) by 1800.

Time Line

1775   June 17: British regulars defeat Patriot forces at the Battle of Bunker Hill.

1776   Virginia Declaration of Rights establishes freedom of worship. Cherokees attack white American settlements in the South.

March 17: British troops and Loyalists evacuate Boston.

July 4: Second Continental Congress approves Declaration of Independence.

August: Patriots start counterattacks on Cherokees in the South.

September 20: British troops occupy New York City.

September 21: Fire destroys much of New York City.

1777   April 26: British raiders destroy much of Danbury, Connecticut.

May and July: Cherokees sign treaties giving up claim to homelands.

September 26: British troops occupy Philadelphia.

1778   July 4–11: British raiders attack several Connecticut towns, burning Fairfield and Norwalk.

1779   September 1–15: Patriots destroy forty Iroquois towns in New York.

1780   Patriot garrison surrenders to British at Charleston, South Carolina.

1781   Patriots attack large Shawnee town in western Pennsylvania.

September 6: British raiders attack and burn much of New London, Connecticut.

1782   April 12: U.S. and British diplomats begin peace talks in Paris, France.

1783   April 26: Last large group of Loyalists leaves New York City for Canada.

September 3: Treaty of Paris officially ends the American Revolution. British army evacuates New York City.

1784   *Empress of China* sails from New York City to China, opening trade between China and United States.

1787   May 25: Constitutional Convention opens in Philadelphia and eventually results in the writing of the U.S. Constitution.

1790   December 21: Samuel Slater opens first textile mill in Pawtucket, Rhode Island.

1791   November 4: Native Americans defeat Patriots in present-day Indiana.

1793   October 21: Eli Whitney introduces the cotton gin.

General Anthony Wayne defeats Native Americans in present-day Ohio.

1794   August 20: Wayne defeats Native Americans at the Battle of Fallen Timbers.

1795   August 3: Native Americans give up their claim to most of Ohio in Treaty of Greenville.

Glossary

barracks: buildings in which soldiers live.

blockade: close off a place to stop people, supplies, vehicles, or ships from getting in and out.

boycott: refuse to do business with a particular business or country in protest at its policies.

brigand: type of thief that takes things by force.

civilian: person who is not in the armed forces.

colony: settlement, area, or country owned or controlled by another nation.

congress: meeting. The name "Congress" was given to the first meetings of delegates from the British colonies and was then adopted as the name of the U.S. legislature when the United States formed a national government.

constitution: document that lays down the basic rules and laws of a nation or organization.

economy: system of producing and distributing goods and services.

epidemic: outbreak of disease that spreads quickly and widely.

evacuate: leave a place because of danger.

export: send goods for sale out of a country.

fifing: playing a fife, which is a small musical instrument like a flute or recorder.

flax: plant grown for its fiber from which linen is made.

frontier: edge of something known or settled. In the early years of the United States, the frontier meant the most westward point of white settlement.

garrison: military post; or the troops stationed at a military post.

importation: bringing of goods for sale into a country.

inflation: increase in amount of circulated money that causes a steep rise in prices.

legislature: group of officials that makes laws.

loot: steal or take things by force.

Loyalist: American who rejected independence and wanted the colonies to remain British.

militia: group of citizens organized into an army (as opposed to an army of professional soldiers, or regulars).

occupy: enter and take control of.

Patriot: American who supported the American Revolution; more generally, a person who is loyal to and proud of his or her country.

shelling: firing explosive shells in an attack on a target.

siege: military operation in which a group of attackers surrounds a target and either attacks it or keeps it trapped in an attempt to force it to surrender.

tax: sum charged by the government on purchases, property ownership, or income and used to pay for public services or the cost of governing.

treason: crime of betraying one's country, for instance by fighting for or helping an enemy during a war.

Further Resources

Books

Carew–Miller, Anna. *Native American Confederacies* (Native American Life). Mason Crest, 2003.

Harper, Judith E. *African Americans and the Revolutionary War* (Journey to Freedom). Child's World, 2000.

Kallen, Stuart A. *Life During the American Revolution* (The Way People Live). Lucent, 2002.

Redmond, Shirley Raye. *Patriots in Petticoats: Heroines of the American Revolution.* Random House, 2004.

Slavicek, Louise Chipley. *Women of the American Revolution* (Women in History). Greenhaven, 2002.

Places to Visit

The Colonial Williamsburg Foundation
P. O. Box 1776
Williamsburg, VA 23187–1776
Telephone: (757) 229-1000

Web Sites

History's Women
www.historyswomen.com
Web site devoted to achievements and biographies of women has a section on early America that includes Revolutionary heroines, such as Abigail Adams.

Joseph Brant (Thayendanegea), Mohawk
www.indians.org/welker/brant.htm
Web site of the American Indian Heritage Foundation offers a biography of Mohawk leader Joseph Brant.

Indians and the American Revolution
www.americanrevolution.org/ind1.html
Online essay about Native Americans during the Revolution by Wilcomb E. Washburn.

Black Loyalists: Our History, Our People
collections.ic.gc.ca/blackloyalists/
Web site of the Black Loyalists Heritage Society in Canada details the story of African American Loyalists and what happened to them after the Revolution.

The King's Royal Yorkers
royalyorkers.ca/distaff.htm
Web site of the King's Royal Yorkers living history group offers information about the experience of women Loyalists.

Index

Johnson, Samuel, 33

Loyalists, 8, 10, 13, 16, 17,
17, 22, 26–31, **27**, **28**, **29**,
31, 34, 38

Marion, Francis, 16, 24
Maryland, 28, 29
Massachusetts, 8, 10, 15, 20,
21, 29, 35
militia and militiamen, 16, 21
Motte, Rebecca, 24

Native Americans, 10, 17,
17, 26, 36–39, **37**, **38**, **39**,
41, 42
New England, 11, 14, 26, 43
New Hampshire, 8, 35
New Jersey, 8, 15, 26, **28**, 35
New York, 8, 14, 15, 16, **25**,
26, 30, 35, 39
New York City, 10, **11**, 13,
16, 30
North, the, 35, 36, 42
North Carolina, 9, 37

Ohio, 39, 42

Patriots, 8, 9, 10, 13, 16, 22,
24, 25, 26, 28, 32, 33,
34, 37
see also armies and
soldiers, Patriot

Pennsylvania, 8, 15, **17**, 20,
21, 26, 27, 28, 29, 35, 37
Philadelphia, **9**, 11, 13, 16,
24, 29
Philipse, Frederick, 30
Pinckney, Harriet, 24

religion, 4, 8, **8**
Rhode Island, 8, 35, 41

St. Clair, Arthur, 42
settlement, white, 36, 37, 42
sickness and disease, 11
sieges, 11
Sierra Leone, 34
slavery and slaves, 15, 19, 32,
33, **33**, 34, 35, **35**, 42,
43, **43**
see also African
Americans
Slater, Samuel, 41
South, the, 15, 16, 19, 26 35,
36, 42, 43, **43**
South Carolina, 16, 19, 22,
24, 26
Sullivan, John, 17

taxes, 24
trade, 5, 7, 11, 24, 36, 40, 41
Treaty of Greenville, 42
Treaty of Paris, 30, 38, 39

United States of America, 4,
15, 29, 30, 34, 39
after the Revolution, 40,
41, **41**, 42, 43
United States Constitution,
4, 40
U.S. military forces, 42

Virginia, 8, **8**, 25, **33**, 34

Washington, George, 16, 24,
33, 40
Wayne, Anthony, 42
West, the, 37
Wheatley, Phillis, 35, **35**
Whitney, Eli, 43
women, 5, **5**, 11, 13, 17, **19**,
20, **24**, **25**, 31
challenges and responsi-
bilities, 5, 18, 19, 20, 21,
22, 23, 24, 25, 42
fears, 13, 18, 22
rights, 5, 15, 19, 41
as informants and spies,
18, 24
status, 18, 19, 21, 23,
25, 42